To my y
friend Ken.

Thanks for being
a blessing to my
life.
Respectfully
[signature]

THE REAL CURE FOR RACISM

REFLECTIONS ON THE MURDER OF GEORGE FLOYD

PASTOR JAMES OWOLABI

DEDICATION

This book is dedicated to my parents who taught me to love God and love people with all my heart, soul, and mind, the Rev. Dr. Solomon Owolabi and Mrs. Christian Owolabi who always opened their home and heart to people around the world because they loved Jesus. They considered themselves citizens of heaven and their children instruments in the hand of God to change the world. "Baba, I miss you every day. I love you so much. Thank you for encouraging me to write this book. "*Mydear*," thanks for loving children.

CONTENTS

PRAISE FOR
THE REAL CURE FOR
RACISM

"Pastor James Owolabi has mentored me for a decade and is one of my best friends. *The Real Cure for Racism* offers the only *real* cure for racism." — Jason Taber, Youth Pastor at The Vail Church

"James is a man whose humility and love for all is contagious. His book is as well. This world is starving for the perspective *The Cure for Racism* provides." — Scott Ziegler, Lead Teaching Pastor of The Bridge Community Church

"Tears welled up in my eyes as I read The Cure for Racism; tears of grief as I recalled the pain you endured due to racism mixed with tears of joy seeing how God works all things together for good. He has called you for

His purpose to bring this message of truth to a world in pain.

When we first met many years ago, I told you that you were an answer to prayer. Little did I know then that we would become family, and little did I know how much I would learn from you. I watched you truly listen to troubled youth and adults, and give them hope, true hope, through faith in Christ Jesus. Reading The Real Cure for Racism reminded me that I need to focus less on the outrage I feel listening to the news and spend more time listening to the Holy Spirit and to hurting souls. Thank you for being a blessing in my life." — Rose McKeown (Your Vanilla Mom)

INTRODUCTION

A worldwide pandemic is caused by an extremely virulent virus that is racing around the globe, affecting every country, every people group, and every age group. The bad news is there is no vaccination for this affliction. The good news is that there is a cure that works 100% of the time when the dose is administered correctly. I know because though I was afflicted by this virus and suffered the symptoms, I ultimately recovered. Here's my story.

Chapter One

MY STORY

*"Whenever we tell God what to do, it never goes
well." – The Indianapolis Pastor
God Used to Wake Me Up*

The events that led to my infection began years
ago when I was called to be the interim pastor at a
church in Elma, Washington. That position was an
incredible culmination for a young man from Nigeria
who had moved to the state of Washington to earn a
seminary degree to work in full-time Christian
ministry. Before moving into this role in Elma, I had
been a youth pastor at a church in Belfair,
Washington, for nine years, where I enjoyed fantastic
love and support. They helped pay for my seminary
training and financially supported my journey in my

immigration issues regarding gaining my permanent status. The love I felt from both churches was beyond anything I could have imagined. In fact, I was so genuinely accepted by these overwhelmingly white congregations that sometimes I forgot I was from Africa. It was clear that they did not see me nor treat me as the stereotypical young black African, but rather as a young man who was passionate about God. Despite this nurturing environment, I was sadly about to turn my back on these loving people because of the actions of a single individual.

One day, a man showed up at the church and asked me to come outside and look in the trunk of his car. When he opened the trunk, I discovered it was full of rocks. He then told me the Lord had instructed him to sell the rocks for $1000 apiece. This man was shaking, eyes were bloodshot red, and he looked quite disoriented. Although he spoke clearly and confidently, he was quite agitated, so I told him he should get some sleep and see a doctor. Upon this advice, he got very upset and left. Three days later, he called the church and called me the N-word in a rant. I figured he had blown off some steam, and that was the end of it. But he kept calling until one day it escalated into a death threat. I called the police and was taken into protective custody. Eventually, the police caught the man who had been seen by my house with a knife threatening to skin the "N-word" alive.

Needless to say, I was greatly shaken by this experience since it was my first taste of outright bigotry and hate in America. Feeling that my church did not empathize enough with my hurt and pain, I foolishly resigned and vowed these three things:

1) Never again will I pastor a church where 80% of the congregation were not of my race.

2) My deep friendships and close relationships would be limited to people who looked like me. Never would I return to the Northwest.

3) Never would I preach to an audience of people who did not look like me.

I moved to Indianapolis, where I got a job at a fast-food restaurant. One day I was providentially and lovingly challenged by a seminary professor, wondering why I was not involved in full-time ministry. At first, I gave him pat answers such as, "God has not yet opened any doors." When he pressed me, I finally admitted I was only interested in an African American church of more than 500 members. His fatherly and pastoral response was a lightning bolt of truth. He reminded me that whenever we tell God what to do, it never goes well. He added that I needed to be willing to go anywhere to any congregation; he basically encouraged me to stop telling God "No". A few days later, I was finally convicted to say to the Lord, "I surrender. Wherever You lead me, I will go." So, I did. Within two months, I was the senior pastor of an English-speaking Korean/American church in Indianapolis.

From this experience of racial mistreatment leading to my disobedience of God and subsequently blaming a particular race for the crime of one man, I'd like to share my ten observations about racism.

Thoughts & Reflections

_____

_____

_____

_____

_____

_____

_____

_____

_____

_____

_____

_____

_____

_____

_____

Chapter Two

SIN IS THE
GREATEST VIRUS

And racism is a symptom…

"What is sin? It is the glory of God not honored.
The holiness of God not reverenced.
The greatness of God not admired. The power of
God not praised. The truth of God not sought. The
wisdom of God not esteemed. The beauty of God not
treasured. The goodness of God not savored.
The faithfulness of God not trusted. The
commandments of God not obeyed.
The justice of God not respected. The wrath of God
not feared. The grace of God not cherished. The
presence of God not prized. The person of God
not loved. That is sin."
— John Piper on What is Sin?

From what I have learned about viruses, they are submicroscopic infectious agents that penetrate a living cell then replicate throughout the body's cells until the entire living being is infected. Funny, that is a perfect picture of what sin does in the human body as well. Viruses corrupt the body; sin corrupts our entire being, spirit, soul, *and* body. Sin's corruption is born in the heart of people twisting the way they think, speak, and behave. Sin is anything contrary to God's Word and His character. God is a Unifier, a Peacemaker, and a loving Father to all of humanity. The nature of sin is the exact opposite. It's a divisive destroyer that hates everything good, right, pure, noble, and of a good report. Sin separates us from God and His predominant attributes.

Like any sickness, some symptoms manifest as a result. With sin, some of the many symptoms include hatred, jealousy, lying, cheating, stealing, manipulating, etc. Racism is an outworking symptom of being separated from God, who embodies love, while racism is the embodiment of hate. And the Bible says that whoever hates his brother hates God (1 John 4:20 & 21). From the beginning, God was clear at creation that every human being is created in His image (Genesis 1:27). We are all descended from the same parents (Romans 4:16). We are all equal in His sight (Galatian 3:28). And He shows NO partiality (Romans 2:11).

Racism is a symptom of sin in the heart of man. While lust is expressed through sexual immorality, adultery, fornication, and the like, racism is expressed through hatred, pride, prejudice, and superiority.

If we want to be rid of racism, we must address the deeper issue of sin in our hearts. I love John Piper's words quoted at the beginning of this chapter because he makes it clear in his definition that sin is the sum of a life devoid of God. Let's examine ourselves today and see where we may be lacking honor, reverence, admiration, truth, wisdom, or esteem. We must repent of those areas and ask the Holy Spirit to help us rid our lives of sin and give us a heart of love for all people.

Thoughts & Reflections

_____

_____

_____

_____

_____

_____

_____

_____

_____

_____

_____

_____

_____

_____

_____

Chapter Three

RACISM IS AN
UNSEEN SYMPTOM

But it is very real.

*"Why has this evil been so difficult to eradicate?
Because racism is not first and foremost a skin
problem. It is a sin problem. See, when you believe
that racism is a skin problem, you can take three
hundred years of slavery, court decisions, marches,
and federal government involvement
and still not get it fixed right.*

*But once you admit that racism is a sin problem,
you are obligated as a believer to deal with it right
away. As long as the issue of race is social and not
spiritual, it will never be dealt with
in any ultimate sense."*

—Dr. Tony Evans on Racism, It's not a Skin Problem, It's a Sin Problem!

No one in their right mind would say that racism does not exist. And we cannot say racism does not exist because we cannot see it. From my experience alone, I know that racism is alive and real, not just in America but in every nation on earth. And it is not merely a black and white issue.

For example, the word "racism" originated in the late 19th Century through a Brigadier General named William Henry Pratt, who oversaw educating the Native Americans in Carlisle, Pennsylvania. In 1902, he was famous for saying, "Kill the Indian, save the man," when speaking about the good it would do for the impoverished Indians to leave their heritage and assimilate into the American culture of their time. Their language was stripped from them; their appearances changed to model what was considered acceptable in society. Basically, they denied their true identity. These types of acts and behaviors have gone on throughout the history of civilization, and generations easily transfer them to other cultures and ethnicities. One group has a prejudice against another group. And it is not always based on the color of our skin; it can be gender, eye color alone, religious beliefs, etc.

We are all prejudiced in some way, form, or fashion. When God clearly tells us in His Word, do not judge, lest you be judged, He will judge you in return with the same measure that you judge (Matthew 7:1—3). Prejudice means to "pre-judge" based on how someone looks, where they come from, their name, color, the way they talk, dress, act, etc. It is not until we encounter Christ and the love of God that we are challenged to let go of these judgments and love people at all costs regardless of who we think they are.

But racism can hide in the hearts of people. On the surface, they seem completely loving, kind, accepting, and supporting, yet when an event occurs where they are forced to make a choice or take a side, foundational beliefs that choose one over another based on ethnicity or skin color may rear its ugly head. Racism can be so deeply rooted in our hearts as part of the sinful nature of human beings that we don't even recognize it. And can be as simple as being born with a selfish nature that demands your way or superiority over others. We are predisposed to be attracted to people who look like us, have the same socioeconomic status as we do, and those things alone can have roots of racism.

Eradicating it from our hearts all goes back to love. Do we love our neighbor as ourselves? Do we love others above ourselves? Will we put their needs above our own? Do we prefer certain types of people while shunning others? These are questions we can ask ourselves to discover the sins that truly lurk deep within our hearts. All to say this, ANY type of sin is ungodly and must be rooted out of our hearts.

Dr. Tony Evans sums this up perfectly, writing, *"We are all from the same root racially. God's agenda for us is that we live in unity with one another, both in the kingdom and in the culture at large."* We need to believe that what God created in humanity was not men and women in their image, but in His image and that diversity of display of His image is perfect and beautiful and worthy of love and honor. In loving and honoring one another, we are ultimately loving and honoring Him, which brings Him the glory due to His name.

Thoughts & Reflections

_____

_____

_____

_____

_____

_____

_____

_____

_____

_____

_____

_____

_____

_____

_____

Chapter Four

RACISM IS NOT
THE BIGGEST PROBLEM

Facing America Today

"It is impossible to meet the real Jesus and be indifferent. You either bow down in wonder or go away offended." – Timothy Keller

We could list all the sins plaguing America today, and racism would only be one listed among them. Let's take a moment for reflection and consider the gravity of the sin problem facing America today. We are a nation marked by the murder of more than 61 million unborn babies. America ranks consistently in the top ten countries that consume the most online pornography. More than half of marriages in America end in divorce.

And worst of all, Christianity has been on the decline in the last decade, with some researchers saying we live in the most biblically illiterate generation in this nation's history. Quite a list for a country that was founded on Judeo-Christian values, and I could go on. Like any other nation, we struggle with greed, lust, pride, envy, wrath, lawlessness, violence, envy, and laziness. And, probably, the biggest problem facing America today is indifference, which simply means a lack of interest, concern, or sympathy. Jesus was quite the contrary to indifferent. He was interested in the lives of people, their wellbeing, their future. He was concerned about their needs, their sicknesses, and their bondage to sin. He had the greatest of sympathy and, when possible, healed them all. His character should be the character of all believers who share the same interests, concerns, and sympathy for humanity regardless of their origins or ethnicity.

Paul told Timothy that in the last days *"men will be lovers of themselves, lovers of money, boastful, arrogant, abusive, disobedient to their parents, ungrateful, unholy, unloving, unforgiving, slander-ous, without self-control, brutal, without love of good, traitorous, reckless, conceited, lovers of pleasure rather than lovers of God, having a form of godliness but denying its power..."* (2 Tim. 3:2—5).

My goodness, this does not sound like the Bride whom Jesus will present to the Father without spot or wrinkle! But Paul's words make it clear that racism is not the biggest problem facing America today; it is one thing only, sin in the hearts of men. It can be quite disheartening to read that list of all the sins that overtake people who are not walking closely with the Lord. And, quite frankly, if a brother or sister is caught up in these sins, it is a natural symptom that they are *not* going to love their neighbor as themselves or put their brother's needs above their own.

Thoughts & Reflections

_____

_____

_____

_____

_____

_____

_____

_____

_____

_____

_____

_____

_____

_____

_____

Chapter Five

THE WORST PART
OF EXPERIENCING RACISM

It can, ironically,

make you a sick racist!

"In a world of selfishness, greed, inequity, and injustice, believers need to be set apart by their consuming love for God and their sacrificial love for others. That's the kind of holy living that brings salt and light to this dark, decaying world."
– John MacArthur on Chaos, Corruption, and the Christian Response

Have you ever noticed that when a particular sin touches you, if it is not dealt with quickly, the sin can take root in your heart? When I experienced racism, as I shared in the beginning, it took a while for me to really deal with the reality of what happened to me. While I recognized what it was, I was not prepared for its effect on my heart and mind. The sin of another person infected my heart, making me sick. Ultimately, I began to think exactly like the racist who targeted me, and it almost cost me all the good and blessings God planned for my life.

I'm reminded of the wise words of Solomon in Proverbs 4:23, *"Guard your heart above all things for out of it spring the issues of life."* When a racist attacked me, my first response should have been to guard my heart. When the people I shared my experience with did not empathize with me, I should have guarded my heart. As my enemy pursued me to destroy me I should have taken the matter to God immediately. He would have defended me like He did the Israelites as Pharaoh's armies pursued. Exodus 14:14, *"The Lord will fight for you; you need only be still."*

I became like a sick racist in response to the hatred and bigotry I experienced through the hands of one man until I had an encounter with another man who God sent to me whose words turned me around. It is best to guard our hearts, give everything to God, and walk on with Him refusing to allow the enemy's tactics to destroy the plan of God for our lives.

Thoughts & Reflections

_____

_____

_____

_____

_____

_____

_____

_____

_____

_____

_____

_____

_____

_____

_____

Chapter Six

RACISM IS NOT THE CURE

to Racism.

"We Christians are called to love our enemies and to suffer injustice rather than return evil for evil (Matt. 5:43–48; Rom. 12:14)." — John Piper, Bloodlines: Race, Cross, and the Christian

Injustices will be done. We must trust God and not our feelings or what we read from media to define how we respond. God is wise, caring and compassionate, sovereign, and in control; we cannot allow our experience to define us. We are being discipled by social media to develop a theology of hatred, and we cannot allow that theology to dominate our minds and hearts. Everybody has a theology, and it affects the way you view God, which affects the way we view people. It also affects how we treat people and how we treat people says more about what we believe about God than anything else. Jesus in his worst moments as a human on the cross decided to offer forgiveness to those who hated him. He did not ignore their evil. Forgiveness means you allow God to show you how to love people and confront evil.

Paul wrote to the Romans, telling them to bless the people who persecuted them. We, too, should bless them and not curse them, which is the way of Christ. We must love and pray for them as Jesus taught us. When we act like Christ, we become door-openers to their conscience so that they can hear and receive the truth, repent, and be converted to Christianity. This is our mission, not to be like the rest of the world that holds judgment and prejudices toward people based on their fundamental God-given human differences but to see the image of God upon them and embrace them as brothers and sisters. God's agenda is fulfilled when we follow His ways.

Racism is a satanic agenda to cause both sides to hate one another and to destroy the fabric of our country

What often happens in the hearts of people riddled with sin is that the effects their sin has on them are projected onto others. Like a person who has been the unfortunate victim often becomes the victimizer, the hated becomes the hater; the unloved become unloving, the rejected becomes the rejector. So, as you can see, people who have been subject to racism often become racists in response.

Racism is not a solution to racism! I tried that, and it doesn't work. This kneejerk response may feel good at the moment and even seems to be right and justified, but it eats away like a poison in the long term. Because of this, the biggest disaster of racism is not racism itself; it's the way it can turn you into a racist. Hate and bitterness will always lose. When a person begins to hate because he or she has been hated on, the result, every time, is a heart of bitterness. This hardening of the heart is also a poison that will wreck a person. The danger of racism-driven hate is that a person can become like the people they are angry about in the first place, which leads to an insidious downward spiral of hate where everyone loses.

You see had I continued in my pattern of racism and developed a hatred for white people and not surrendered to God, I would have developed a hatred and bitterness in life. So, in our world of turmoil, chaos, and lawlessness over racism, we cannot, in turn, become prejudiced toward any other race of people. We cannot judge an entire segment of society over the actions of a few. Yes, there are racists, but not all law enforcement officers are racists, and not all people are racists. We must do as Jesus would do, and that is love all people, even our enemies. The people who do not love us, we must love them with the love of God even more.

Thoughts & Reflections

_____

_____

_____

_____

_____

_____

_____

_____

_____

_____

_____

_____

_____

_____

— Chapter Seven —

LOVE WILL

ALWAYS WIN

Every single time!

*"Love is helping people toward the greatest beauty,
the highest value, the deepest satisfaction, the most
lasting joy, the biggest reward, the most wonderful
friendship, and the most overwhelming worship—
love is helping people toward God."*
– John Piper, Let the Nations Be Glad!
The Supremacy of God in Missions

God is love. He created the universe because He loves. He created man and woman because He loves. He gave us a beautiful place to live because of His love. God created and gave out of His immense, immeasurable love. He gave His Son to die because He loves. Jesus is the expression of God's love and friend. You and I should also be the expression of His love.

Love is the antithesis of sin. Right? Jesus said, "If you love me, you will keep my commands" (John 14:15). You will obey Me. You will love because I am love, and I have created you in love to love, and because you love Me, you will love others as you love Me. It is the kind of love that wins, and make no mistake about it. God's love will unequivocally win in the end. But we must accept His love and walk in His love and extend His love to ALL if we are to win with Him.

Love is the antidote for racism. When we love the way God created us to love, we will not allow any form of racism, prejudice, or superiority to remain in our hearts and minds.

According to Paul's beautiful discourse to the Ephesians, we are to be rooted and grounded in love and able to comprehend the breadth and depth of

God's love, which is the one thing that fills us to the fullness of God. His love is truly a love we cannot comprehend, yet as we learn and grow in His love, we are able to rise above the sins of mankind into our place of the royal priest where we can be like Joseph, the agent of deliverance for our own people or nation. In other words, we will have the answers they seek or the words that will calm the storms of racism when we are confronted with the enemy's blows that try to destroy the plans of God.

God's love will always win!

Thoughts & Reflections

_____

_____

_____

_____

_____

_____

_____

_____

_____

_____

_____

_____

_____

_____

Chapter Eight

HATE WILL ALWAYS LOSE

Every single time!

"Darkness cannot drive out darkness, only light can do that. Hate cannot drive out hate, only love can do that." – Dr. Martin Luther King Jr.

There is an appointed day in this dispensation of time when hate will be utterly defeated and wiped completely away from humanity, along with every other sin, including racism. I am looking forward to that day, and even now, think of the rejoicing that will occur when God's people will no longer be subjected to hatred in people's hearts. But for now, hate cannot exist in a Kingdom that is filled with light, love, peace, joy, and righteousness.

God's people, His ambassadors, represent God's kingdom on earth, which means we are to manifest heaven on earth as long as we are here. Hate, and every other sin, must bow and should not be allowed to exist where we live and operate. But, if we are not aware of the power we possess and the release of heaven, we can propagate through prayer and proclamation. We will allow hate to coexist with all the goodness of God. As the Church, we must rise and take our place to push back these social ills that horribly massacre innocent people.

Hate is a looser, and those who unknowingly allow it to take root in their hearts will ultimately lose the battle they fight, sometimes even thinking they are doing God's service. Like Saul of Tarsus, who thought persecuting Christians was a good, godly thing. But he got a wake-up call on the Road to Damascus by the goodness and grace of God when he learned he was not persecuting men but Christ. Paul had hatred towards God's people in his heart because he did not understand who Jesus Christ of Nazareth was. He did not believe Jesus was the

Messiah, so those who followed Him, Saul thought, were blasphemers and violators of the Law that the Pharisees would not tolerate. Their sentence was death in his eyes. He hated them and thought he loved God but discovered he was on the wrong side.

God hates the things that hurt humanity, sin. Solomon listed seven heart conditions in Proverbs 6:16—19 that God detests, and, interestingly, all of them are demonstrated by how we treat others. The list includes:

1) Pride
2) Lying
3) Shedding innocent blood
4) Hearts that devise evil plans
5) People who are swift while running to evil
6) A false witness
7) People who sow discord or division

When Solomon wrote Proverbs 6, he listed six things that God hates and a seventh sin God detests. All the sins listed are demonstrated by a person filled with hate, but the most detestable one is sowing discord among the brethren. God hates division, and frankly, He desires that Christians detest it as well. As Paul wrote, we should be the peacemakers, the unifiers that endeavor to keep unity in the bond of peace.

Hate always loses because love alone will win! And God is love!

For anyone who hates they will ultimately discover they were on the wrong side of God. While we watch injustice unfold and see the horrific effects of sin in the hearts of men played out, we must know that God alone is Judge. He hates no one; He desires them to come to know Christ. He hates sin because sin destroys the hearts of people. So, we can easily surmise that God "hates hate" because hate destroys humanity, both the innocent and the guilty alike.

Please remember this, "Hatred will always stir up strife, but love covers every offense" (Proverbs 10:12). Hate will always lose, so allow the Holy Spirit to search your heart today and remove any residues of hatred, repent, and be made brand new.

Since light is the only thing that can drive out darkness and love, the only thing that can drive out hatred, let us love and love like God and Christ, without condition and measure. For then, we will be the true reflection of Jesus to the world.

Thoughts & Reflections

_____

_____

_____

_____

_____

_____

_____

_____

_____

_____

_____

_____

_____

_____

_____

Chapter Nine

BITTERNESS IS NOT
THE CURE

"I choose love. No occasion justifies hatred. No injustice warrants bitterness. I choose love. Today I love God and what God loves." – Max Lucado

When racism or hatred or bigotry, or any sin is not dealt with in the heart, the result is bitterness. The Bible has much to say about the dangers of bitterness. A root of bitterness will defile many (Hebrews 12:15). It should be put away from us, along with wrath, anger, clamor, and slander (Ephesians 4:31). Bitterness can completely overtake you filling your mouth with curses (Romans 3:14).

As you can see, bitterness will take you places you never want to go to. And, when you are bitter, you infect others with your bitter words and actions. Hebrew 12:15 is an excellent example of this; your bitterness will defile many. When you stand before God, you will get the replay of just how destructive your bitterness was to your family, friends, church, community, coworkers, and everyone else you touched. It will not be pretty, but ugly to God.

Bitterness will also make you sick spirit, soul, and body, creating a life of waste and sadness. In the end, the only things a bitter person truly desires are love and peace. Somewhere along the way, they were denied both, then decided to consciously choose bitterness as a way of life. Reject bitterness today. It is not the cure. It will not bring you the hopes and dreams you have long abandoned as you get stuck in a pattern of self-destruction. And, God has so much more for you, plans of peace, to give you hope and a future that is completely free from bitterness of any kind.

We must replace bitterness with the love of God that covers all sin. Our sin as well as the sin of others. And love takes no account of a suffered wrong. It washes the slate clean and erases it every time another blow comes. This type of response to sin reminds me of Stephen, who was stoned to death. Both he and Jesus, when near death, said the same words, *"Forgive them Lord they do not know what they are doing"* (Luke 23:24 and Acts 7:60). We need to get hold of this truth. We are here for the benefit of our enemies, for the benefit of those who use and abuse us, for those who persecute us.

In "Life Together: The Classic Exploration of Community," Dietrich Bonhoeffer wrote, *"Jesus Christ lived in the midst of his enemies. At the end all his disciples deserted him. On the Cross he was utterly alone, surrounded by evildoers and mockers. For this cause he had come, to bring peace to the enemies of God. So, the Christian, too, belongs not in the seclusion of a cloistered life but in the thick of foes. There is his commission, his work. 'The kingdom is to be amid your enemies. And he who will not suffer this does not want to be of the Kingdom of Christ; he wants to be among friends, to sit among roses and lilies, not with the bad people but the devout people. O you blasphemers and betrayers of Christ! If Christ had done what you are doing who would ever have been spared' (Luther)."*

Think of his words, "The Christian belongs in the thick of foes." We want to run from our foes, and tragically we become bitter in our hiding rather than staying in the fray, walking with them in love, and showing them a way of life saturated with forgiveness and grace. We don't want to be a Christians who refuse to be among the sinners; we want to be right there in the middle of the darkness holding out our hands toward the one who hates us.

Bonhoeffer went on to write, *"Nothing can be more cruel than the leniency which abandons others to their sin. Nothing can be more compassionate than the severe reprimand which calls another Christian in one's community back from the path of sin."*

We must begin to understand how God works among sinners. He prefers mercy to judgment, but mercy cannot be meted out until truth is known, and truth cannot be known where there is no self-reflection of the heart. When we live in the middle of our foes, we walk as an aroma of life and death. Bitterness brings death; love brings life. We are the road sign of Jesus, who continually points the bitter ones to a better way of love in Christ. They will never see that, though, if we refuse to be among them.

We need the only thing that can cure racism. And we must be ready and willing to put our flesh to death when injustices arise. We must refuse offense of any kind. Guard your heart, repent, and forgive quickly, stay close to Christ because, in the end, He is our only hope to be cured of racism and all types of sin.

Thoughts & Reflections

Chapter Ten

CHRIST IS THE REAL CURE TO RACISM

"May the Gospel of Jesus Christ scrape every last shred of racism out of our hearts. Let's start sharing this message across the street, across the tracks and across the world! Only through the Gospel can racism be cured!"

– Jack Stier, Founder of Dare to Share and Author of the upcoming "Unlikely Fighter"

There is only ONE CURE for Racism – Christ!

Jack Stier's testimony of his entire family's deliverance from racism and violence has been repeated time and time throughout history from nations and peoples around this world. His story of redemption is exactly what God wants for all of humanity.

The Stier's were the only white family in the middle of a predominantly Mexican part of the city known for high crime rates and bloodshed in North Denver. He says his family was notoriously violent, and organized crime leaders often referred to his father and uncles as "the crazy brothers." Racism was real, and Jack was raised with an "us" versus "them" mentality that resulted in intense hatred.

One day a preacher went to his toughest, angriest Uncle Jack and led him to the Lord. Jack says, "Jesus came in and changed everything." One by one, his family members came to Christ. His Uncle Bob was born-again in the back of a squad car after beating a man to death who was later resuscitated. Jack remembers being a witness to the transformation of his family as the Holy Spirit washed the slime of racism away.

Jack wrote, *"Soon my family members were side by side in church with their Latino brothers and sisters in Christ. It took time. It was messy. There were slip ups. But the trajectory of their transformation from racism to love was shockingly obvious to me and to everyone who truly knew my family. So what are the implications of all this? Simply that the cure to racism in our hearts is Jesus and the cure to racism on our streets is the church."*

Christ is the only thing that can wipe the sin of racism away; a relationship with Him filters hatred into love.

Jesus died on The Cross to deliver humanity from racism. Though we still possess the sins or wounds of racism, He has already made way for deliverance and healing. We must understand one thing, as long as we live in a fallen world, there will be people who have not encountered the living Christ – His death and resurrection, His victory over sin, sickness, and death – who do not have a revelation of righteousness, love, peace, and joy. They have not been exposed to the truth nor experienced the power and presence of our loving God who desires mercy over judgment!

We must remember this because, as God's representatives on the earth, we are the ones who are anointed and called to be the voice of reason amid turmoil, chaos, and lawlessness. We are the ones who were created to point people to Christ. We have the answer, the antidote, that is needed in our nation today. But our words need to be seasoned with salt and spoken with grace so that mercy will be meted out over judgment.

We must also be like the sons of Issachar, who know the times and seasons. We must know the heart of God and the great plan He has for humanity. If Christ is the only cure and He IS, then our job is not to get consumed by the sin, by the racism, but by the love of God to preach the Gospel, to release the better way to freedom in Christ. Let us not get caught up in man's debates but heaven's decrees. Let us be God's agents of deliverance, soldiers of love, with weapons of mercy and grace.

It's time to get onto the side of God, to walk with Him, and be like Christ. Because friends, He is the ONLY cure for the sin of racism in the hearts of people.

Thoughts & Reflections

_____

_____

_____

_____

_____

_____

_____

_____

_____

_____

_____

_____

_____

_____

_____

Chapter Eleven

REFLECTIONS ON RACISM

And George Floyd's Murder

"Recent racially charged incidents including the tragic death of George Floyd have stirred ensuing riots and torn open the rawest of wounds – racism. Judging a person according to skin color is an ancient sin. For that reason, God gave this ancient solution. In the earliest words of Scripture, God spoke: "Let us make human beings in our image, make them reflecting our nature so they can be responsible for the fish in the sea, the birds in the air, the cattle, and, yes, Earth itself, and every animal that moves on the face of Earth"
(Genesis 1:26).

Embedded in these words is the most wonderful of promises: God made us to reflect his image." – Max Lucado on What is the answer to Racism? This profound yet simple promise!

It was not a regular event: it was a strategic satanic attack against the fabric of America, designed to divide America and the American family. Satan intends, even now, to destroy the academic institutions in America. The murder was pure evil. There was nothing right or justified about it. I'm reminded that our God specializes in using the darkest moments of our lives as the greatest way of communicating His grace, truth, and love, just like the cross of Jesus was the darkest event in the Christian story. God used that evil satanic event for the salvation and redemption of his church.

Our response to the George Floyd murder should be three-fold:

1) Admit that racism exists in America.
2) Accept that we cannot do anything to change it because it is a heart issue.

3) Allow God to use us as His mouthpiece of grace and truth to change the hearts and minds of people.

ONLY GOD can change the heart of a racist.

I am a proud American. I am also a proud Christian. However, I am a Christian first. My belief in the Bible must be the filter through which I view and interpret reality. I refuse to allow any event, even the murder of a black man, to hijack my theology. Racism is real and prevalent in America and is present in people from all races across the world. But it is not just an American problem. It is as old as humanity's existence itself. And has touched every tongue and tribe of people.

I love America but am afraid for my dear country after the murder of George Floyd. I am also afraid for the American church. We have lost our theological minds and have allowed our hearts to be molded by slogans from social media. The murder of George Floyd was satanic and demonic. The murder of George Floyd crushed my heart in many ways, but it also reminded me that evil is present, and the devil is working overtime to destroy the fabric of faith in God. It traumatized me and made me question the goodness of God and reaffirmed the doctrine of total depravity.

George Floyd was killed by a murderer! He was killed not just because that police officer was racist; he was a cold-hearted, godless sinner. The DNA of the devil was prevalent on the murder scene. We must not subject ourselves to watching this satanic act of violence over and over as some would have us do. It was pure evil, dark, and satanic. The officer was a demonic agent who did not grasp that he was made in God's image with a duty to protect and serve and, more significantly, that George Floyd also was made in God's image.

As Max Lucado so eloquently wrote in the article quoted above, if we would remember that all people are made in the image of God, we would handle people with God's care and love. Pastor Lucado went on to give a pertinent answer to a very important question. He asked, *"What is God's solution to angry racism that gives birth to violence and bloodshed? Government programs might help. Lectures might enlighten. But, in the end, God's plan is the only plan: see every person on the planet as God's idea. And He has no bad ideas."*

Let me be honest! The injustice of racism is not unique to America. In my native country of Nigeria and all over Africa, police brutality is rampant, and hardly anything can get done without bribing the police. I mentioned this to point out that the virus of sin is a global phenomenon, and yelling slogans about how Blue or Black Lives Matter is not the solution. The answer is to allow God to change hearts and minds radically. I've learned many other truths from my experience that I'll briefly touch on here in this short essay but will expound upon later in my book on human flourishing and the preciousness of human life.

I want to expound a little more on my thoughts about love and hate. To be clear, loving God and loving people are not easy, but it is the greatest vaccine against the virus of sin, which has the symptoms of racism. Learning to love people is hard work. It is easy to be indifferent towards people. It is easier to show indifference than to show love. It is easier to be indifferent than to hate someone. The key against this virus is to allow the love of God to overwhelm our minds and explode into our hearts. Love is not the opposite of hate; love is the opposite of indifference. To combat this attitude of indifference, we need to focus on two key activities: first, to listen to what a person from another culture is saying, and second, to learn about that person. Knowing and understanding someone is the remedy for indifference and the catalyst for love, where the goal then is to discover how to serve best those who are different.

Finally, I've concluded we cannot fix racism nor eradicate racism from the hearts of humanity, which is not fatalism. It is merely a fact that until Christ returns, racism will exist simply because it is a Satanic, selfish perspective on life; racism is the result of sinful hearts. But this global pandemic of racism has a bright spot. The cure is available to every person who honestly and earnestly seeks it. I discovered that when I allowed Christ to change me with His message and lifestyle; to change the way I dealt with people, the racism I was harboring in my heart melted away. Imagine this change happening to hundreds of thousands, if not millions, of people worldwide who are afflicted with sin that leads to racism. Yes, Christ is the answer! Look into the pages of the Bible and look at Jesus Christ, especially in the gospels and allow him to change your heart, and you will love like no one else. God bless you!

Thoughts & Reflections

_____

_____

_____

_____

_____

_____

_____

_____

_____

_____

_____

_____

_____

_____

— Chapter Twelve —

ONLY GOD

"If you're spending more time discussing CRT than you are KRT, then you've been tricked by the world. Now in Christ, there are new rules.
And if you will abide by the new rules of Christ, we will create something new. So, while they're fighting out there, we have peace in here. Because we're operating on one new man." – Dr. Tony Evans on Kingdom Race Theory

Only God can change a racist's heart and mind and then heal the heart of one who has been affected by the evil and injustice of racism. He alone can change the mistrust that has been built into low-income families and the justice system in America. Only He can heal the pain that we all have experienced from events like 9/11, George Floyd's murder, or the wars of the last twenty years.

Amid such uncertainty and the opportunity to be overcome by worry and fear, God has chosen to use instruments of His peace in a constantly more chaotic world. Darkness is filling the earth, and people are becoming increasingly angry and bitter. Only God can give us the wisdom to know how to live as a country of immigrants and children of immigrants. Remember, we are citizens of heaven only sojourning through this life. We must lean into the word of God so that we can receive His direction.

Today we are hearing about a theory being taught within the institutions of America from elementary school through higher education; in the military and corporate America. It's called Critical Race Theory (CRT). Right after George Floyd's murder, Tony Evans delivered a sermon to his Dallas congregation about why CRT is so polarizing and why we need to adopt a different perspective of racial matters based on God's Word alone and not the opinions of men. His message brought clarity, where the discussion over CRT has brought confusion. Several groups have hijacked the original intent of the theory to further their agendas, whether to support Black Lives Matter, the 1619 Project, police violence, or reparations. Either way, none are focused on the one answer, Christ, or the wisdom that comes from the Word of God.

First, I want you to understand what CRT is and where it came from in history. Let me start by assuring you. It is not a brand-new idea that has suddenly sprung upon American institutions over the last year. CRT is a post-civil-rights social construct that seeks to demonstrate how the embedded foundation and filter of racist attitudes, behaviors, policies, and structures have been rooted throughout the fabric of America and American life, and in social systems, even after civil rights laws were enacted. To put this in historical context, the Civil Rights Acts were passed and implemented in 1964. While much has changed since the days of Jim Crow Laws and the segregation and separation they brought, there still lie within the fabric of our culture racial undertones and prejudices that have their roots in old mindsets about racial differences.

Dr. Tony Evans proposed, and many have adopted, what he termed the "Kingdom Race Theory" (KRT) based solely on Paul's writings to the church at Ephesus about the character of God and the qualities that Christians should demonstrate to their families, neighbors, community, etc. He defined KRT as *"the reconciled recognition, affirmation, and celebration of the divinely created ethnic differences through which God displays his multifaceted glory, as his people justly, righteously and responsibly function personally, and corporately, in unity under the lordship of Jesus Christ."*

Christians must be people of the truth. We are not people of color; we are children of God with a completely different identity than those who do not know Him. He expects us to live by, relate to, and learn the truth that comes from His Word alone, not from social constructs or man's theories that produce division and ultimate destruction in the human heart.

Dr. Evans used Paul's words in Ephesians 2:11-22 to demonstrate what Paul has to say to the believing Jews and Gentiles about their common faith in Christ to remind them that being a Jew does not make anyone greater and that circumcision is not a mark of higher faith or spirituality. In other words, the Christians of the Ephesian church were dividing themselves based on ethnic origins and traditions, behaviors that were not to be participated in by Christ-followers. Paul is correcting them and telling them there's a new way, as Dr. Evans put it, a *"Cristo-centric way."*

> *"Therefore, remember that you, once Gentiles in the flesh—who are called Uncircumcision by what is called the Circumcision made in the flesh by hands— that at that time you were without Christ, being aliens from the commonwealth of Israel and strangers from the covenants of promise, having no hope and without God in the world. But now in Christ Jesus you who once were far off have been brought near by*

the blood of Christ.

*For He Himself is our peace, **who has made both one, and has broken down the middle wall of separation**, having abolished in His flesh the enmity, that is, the law of commandments contained in ordinances, so as to create in Himself one new man from the two, thus making peace, and that He might reconcile them both to God in one body through the cross, thereby putting to death the enmity. And He came and preached peace to you who were afar off and to those who were near. For through Him we both have access by one Spirit to the Father.*

Now, therefore, you are no longer strangers and foreigners, but fellow citizens with the saints and members of the household of God, having been built on the foundation of the apostles and prophets, Jesus Christ Himself being the chief cornerstone, in whom the whole building, being fitted together,

> *grows into a holy temple in the Lord, in whom you also are being built together for a dwelling place of God in the Spirit."*

Christ has broken the middle wall of separation; let's not re-erect it and play into the enemy's hand by allowing division and strife to destroy us. We are to do as Christ did, to come to unity in faith and walk together, seeing no differences or divisions among us. We are family, and our homeland is heaven, a place with no division or separation.

Even so, it is human nature to always look at the outward man. I remember what happened when Samuel went to Jesse's house to anoint the next king. David's father didn't think enough of him to call him in from the sheepfold. His brothers didn't think much of him either, and they mocked him when he showed up with their lunch then slew the giant that the armies of God were hiding from in fear. Even God knew our tendencies to look at outward differences. Unless we purpose our hearts to see as God sees, we will judge every time based on looks, dress, status, etc. Only

God can change our hearts and minds so we will see as He sees, the hearts of one another and of those we are called to bring God's peace and salvation to all.

As we learn to practice Dr. Evans' Kingdom Race Theory of walking in unity in the bond of peace, we will not only hold the door open for God to transform us into the image of Christ but for God to transform others as well.

The bottom line, Christians ought to be the most loving, most unifying force on this planet. We ought to be bringing peace to every disagreement. We ought to have God's wisdom and truth flowing from our lips into every aspect of our culture.

We need a Kingdom mindset; the eyes, ears, mouth, and heart of Christ. We need to celebrate our differences and the beauty of God's multifaceted glory that rests upon His people. It's time to unify and let God's love be seen and known upon all of us, so the entire world will recognize that we are indeed Christ's disciples.

Thoughts & Reflections

— Chapter Thirteen —

BUILD AND BE

THE BRIDGE

As my apprehension culminated regarding everything I saw on the media, I discovered the anecdote for racism while driving through the South for a speaking engagement. I'd always heard about the prejudices of the South, but God had planned an event that would change my preconceived notions.

In Kentucky, I stopped to fill my gas tank. As I pulled up to the pump, a police officer stopped right in front of me. I have to admit I immediately became concerned. Thoughts of all my past experiences and what could be were running through my mind all at once. Was this officer about to question me and ask me where I was going? Would he harass me? Nervously, I walked toward the store door, and I was shocked to see the officer run ahead of me to open the door. As I approached, he opened the door, bowed, and asked me to go ahead of him.

An absolutely astounding conversation followed where we sat down, talked together about our lives and families, sharing a few minutes of fellowship with smiles and well wishes before leaving. It  would become a moment that changed my perspective of people who lived in the South, police officers, what matters most, and makes the difference in a world where many are on edge over the media's relentless rhetoric regarding racism.

I also recognized that I had to make a choice that day not to allow my past to affect my present. As a result, my interaction with this Police Officer blew my mind.

Over the past year, since George Floyd was murdered, we've allowed the media to affect our thoughts and opinions about racism in America rather than turning to God for direction as to how we can bring healing and restoration to broken relationships. I contemplated the affect these events have had on people and asked God to give me wisdom. I needed to know what to do in this season of time and He gave me a vision. I believe Christians are to be a bridge between divergent views of different people groups. Bridges that make a way of reconciliation possible. The media's reporting forces people to take a side, but when you become a bridge, you provide a pathway through both sides of the issue.

Jesus is the Great Bridge, Isaiah prophesied about Jesus calling Him the *repairer of the breach* (Is. 58:12). He knew how to reconcile, in fact, He came to reconcile us to the Father. It was His purpose. And, we have each received His ministry of reconciliation according to 2 Corinthians 5:18. To be a bridge, we must learn to sacrifice our tendencies to pre-judge people. We must learn to be kind, listen, learn, and love.

Jesus is our perfect example. He built a bridge for the woman at the well, Nicodemus, the lepers, and the woman caught in adultery. We need only to study Jesus' interactions with these people to see exactly how we can be a bridge for the people God places in our lives.

First, if we want to allow God to bring reconciliation, we must **build a bridge** with people who don't look like us. It will take dedication, effort, and time. We will have to finish what we've started. The hard labor will be worth it. You will be working on both sides of the issue, so there may be some days you want to quit before you bring your bridge to completion. Don't quit! Stay focused on what God desires and keep building until you have connected both sides.

Secondly, we must *be the bridge*. When we choose to build and be the bridge, we must be okay with being misunderstood and maligned for our efforts to bring reconciliation. Don't pay attention to the naysayers and mockers. Know that you are on God's assignment, continuing the work of Christ to bring restoration and wholeness to people. Our goal should not be racial reconciliation but repairing the breach between people and God.

And, thirdly, we must *strengthen the bridge*. Bridges can fall apart. Even after we build the bridge, we will have to repair it regularly. Christians, even churches, are tired of the conversation about racism. They are tired of being called a racist or judging those on either side of the issue. People want to be understood. They want peace. So, once the bridge is built, we will have to put a lot of effort into bringing the two sides together for conversation. We will have to put out fires and bring understanding to disagreements and unity to division. Each is a part of strengthening the bridge; nothing can be overlooked.

During our efforts, we should never ignore the best Builder, God. Like Abraham, we must also look for a city with foundations, whose builder and maker is God (Hebrews 11:10). The city's foundation is Christ, the cornerstone, upon whom we build. We repair, we raise up generations of people who have been divided over an issue that God simply does not see. He sees no color, He sees beauty in His creation, and we too must see as He sees and build as He builds…with grace. Jesus himself is the bridge of grace; and we too, as His partner and co-laborers, are to be that bridge of grace.

While building, being, and maintaining our bridge, we must remember a few essential character traits of those who successfully bring reconciliation to both sides of the bridge.

1) Connect before you correct
2) Be humble
3) Learn the language
4) Value and respect people
5) Serve people

Love is the license to speak, and you cannot love

someone if you don't connect heart-to-heart with them first. While people on both sides of the bridge will need correction, do not be tempted to share it before the real love connection is established. Otherwise, you will tear down the bridge you spent so much time building. You will leave people offended, worse yet, wounded, and the entire building process will have to start all over again.

I cannot say enough about being humble. God gives grace to the humble, which will empower you as you bring reconciliation to others. Humble people submit to leaders and elders looking for a way to wholeness; they ask questions to understand. As you humble yourself, God will give you favor and open doors to bring unity to both sides of your bridge.

We cannot relate to people when we do not understand their language. To understand, we must listen and learn, listen to their hearts, and hear their words. The value of listening cannot be understated here. As we listen, understanding comes, then we can release the answers and wisdom God gives us as we endeavor to bridge the gap between people.

We must value and respect people. If you've built that bridge, I know you already value the people since you are trying to repair relationships and bring unity. Don't allow disruptions or rocky roads to alter your posture toward the people. Even if your endeavor seems to fail in the beginning, don't give up. Keep trying to bring restoration any way the Lord shows you. Your efforts will eventually be rewarded with victory from the Lord!

Finally, serve people! Jesus was a servant to all. He bent down humbly and washed the feet of His disciples. Don't be afraid to do the same exact thing with those you are trying to influence. When you serve others, you win them completely to Christ and reconcile them to God. Service connects them. At one time in history, the church tore down walls by serving people. They built schools and hospitals, and both were tools of service. You can't build without serving people. As you serve them, fear is numbed, and hate dissipates.

Cultural barriers are broken by serving others, and the virus of racism will be isolated, paralyzed, and ultimately destroyed.

As I mentioned in the beginning of this book, the bad news is there is no vaccination for racism. The good news is that there is a cure that works 100% of the time when the dose is administered correctly. The cure... God alone! We all must turn away from our sins, repent, and make Jesus the Lord of our life.

As we surrender to Him, the Holy Spirit will start the transformation process bringing us step-by-step to the image and likeness of Christ. We will speak, act, and love just like Him. We will be healed and free from all prejudices, preconceived notions, and urges to discriminate against people who don't look or act like us. We will truly become like Jesus the repairer of the breach.

Today I pray for you. *May you be filled to the full knowledge of Christ knowing the hope of your calling and your destiny to fulfill that ministry of reconciliation God has given to you. May you build bridges far and wide, becoming the deliverer of people and families, communities and regions, states, and nations around the world. May YOU fulfill the work of an evangelist and turn the world upside down for Christ. In the mighty name of Jesus, I pray, amen!*

Thoughts & Reflections

_____

_____

_____

_____

_____

_____

_____

_____

_____

_____

_____

_____

_____

_____

_____

_____

Endnotes:

https://www.foxnews.com/opinion/max-lucado-answer-racism-profound-simple-promise-max-lucado

https://gregstier.org/a-cure-for-racism/

ABOUT THE AUTHOR

James Owolabi is an evangelist, church planter, and educator who currently lives in Nigeria. He was born and raised in Africa, then spent the first twenty years of his adult life in full-time ministry in the United States. He served in the youth ministry for over two decades in North America.

Owolabi is also one of the teaching pastors at a multi-site church in the Chicago area. James is a second-generation ordained Baptist Minister who is passionate about building churches, schools, and leaders in Africa.

Connect with Pastor James Owolabi at: www.jamesowolabi.com

CPSIA information can be obtained
at www.ICGtesting.com
Printed in the USA
LVHW081919121221
705961LV00001B/18